EVERY MARRIAGE CAN WORK

Remi Oluyale

Unless otherwise indicated, all scripture quotations in this book are from the King James Version (KJV) of the Bible.

EVERY MARRIAGE CAN WORK!
Copyright © 2016 Remi Oluyale
ISBN: 978-37718-1-7

Printed by CreateSpace

All rights reserved. No portion of this publication may be used without the express written consent of the publisher.

DEDICATION

Dedicated to all couples who will believe with me that: Every Marriage Can Work!

CONTENT

	Introduction	7
1.	What is marriage?	11
2.	God's purpose for marriage	17
3.	Satan on the attack	25
4.	Seven reasons why every marriage can work	39
5.	What helps marriage to work	61
6.	Consequences of a dysfunctional marriage	67
7.	Conflict resolution	73
8.	What is love?	81
9.	The duties of a husband	91
10.	The duties of a wife	107
11.	How to change your spouse	113
12.	Rekindling love	117

INTRODUCTION

"He said unto them, Moses because of the hardness of your hearts suffered you to put away your wives: but from the beginning it was not so." (Matt. 19:8)

Is there any hope for the family? With the rate of divorce and broken homes rising everyday in modern society, is it still possible to live happily ever after? What has become of the traditional family virtues of the past? Even Christian families are not spared in this hordes-of-hell's march against the family.

Are broken homes, broken hearts and broken children the price to pay for modernization? If that is so, then what is

Every Marriage Can Work

the hope of our modern society? What does the future hold for future generations? Families are units of the society. If society is going to get sane, then family units must be put back on track.

Christians are the light of the world. Without us, the world is in the dark. We are to show illumination to the hearts of the dying world. An example of a peaceful and successful Christian home is enough gospel to the world. The world wants to see the Prince of peace in our homes, not only on our lips.

Jesus Christ answered the Pharisees saying: "From the beginning, it was not so". Is it still possible for us to go back to the beginning? Can families still be peaceful just as God intended it to be?

My burden is to see every Christian couple stay happily married. I will be sharing with you in this book, some principles from the word of God, researches and personal revelations that I believe will help you live happily thereafter with your spouse. I have taught some of these principles both at home and abroad with diverse testimonies abounding. To the glory of God, I have seen

Introduction

marriages turn around for the better and separated relationships restored. I have seen long lost smiles returning into homes. Many pastors are also now teaching these principles and I am receiving e-mails of testimonies to the glory and the praise of the name of the Lord.

As you read this book, I am certain that your marital relationship will get better. If you are already thinking of packing it up, just pause a little bit and go through this book. I believe your marriage shall be saved. If you are not yet married, this is the very time you need to learn before you enter into marriage. You have a great opportunity in your hands!

CHAPTER ONE

What is marriage?

The word "marriage" sends shivers down the spine of many. It is unbelievable to know that a good percentage of the unmarried are already afraid of marriage even before choosing a life partner! Some married people, because of the experiences they've had in marriage, only remember woes when the word "marriage" is mentioned. Many often simply feel uneasy at the mention of the word "marriage" because of their own personal guilt resulting from their unfaithfulness to their spouses.

What is marriage? Is marriage a "necessary evil" as defined by some? Is marriage something to be desired? Is it a good thing or just something to be tolerated for as long as it is tolerable?

Every Marriage Can Work

I will define marriage simply as a union between a man and a woman in holy matrimony. It is a life time commitment between a man and a woman with a legal back up.

"Therefore shall a man leave his father and his mother, and shall cleave unto his wife and they shall be one flesh." (Gen. 2:24)

Marriage according to God's word is not a union between two people of the same sex. Therefore, homosexuality and lesbianism are perversions.

"For this cause God gave them up unto vile affections: for even their women did change the natural use into that which is against nature: And likewise also the men, leaving the natural use of the woman, burned in their lust one toward another; men with men working that which is unseemly, and receiving in themselves that recompense of their error which was meet. And even as they did not like to retain God in their knowledge, God gave them over to a reprobate mind, to do those things

What Is Marriage?

which are not convenient;.........Who knowing the judgement of God, that they which commit such things are worthy of death, not only do the same, but have pleasure in them that do them." (Rom.1:26-28, 32)

God frowns at such heinous sins and that was the reason why Sodom and Gomorrah were burnt with fire. Homosexuals and lesbians are preparing their souls for eternal fire unless they have a change of heart and salvation in Christ.

Marriage is also not a union between a man and two or more women or a woman and two or more men. Marriage as God ordained it is necessarily a union between a man and a woman. Marriage is a good thing to be desired:

"And the Lord God said, it is not good that the man should be alone, I will make him an help meet for him." (Gen.2:18)

Marriage is Good

Marriage is good. It is to remain alone that the Lord God said was not good for Adam. Marriage is not to be feared.

Every Marriage Can Work

It is to be desired. Everything God created was good, and so is the marriage institution. No matter how people had defined marriage according to their personal experiences, marriage can still be what God says it is in your own life if only you can go about it God's way.

Undefiled Bed
Marriage as God ordained it must be with an undefiled bed.

"Marriage is honourable in all, and the bed undefiled: but whoremongers and adulterers God will judge." (Heb.13:4)

For marriage to be honourable, the bed must be undefiled. Marriages with defiled bed are marriages without divine honour. It is better to graduate into marriage with honours.

Two Types of Marriages
There are two types of first or original marriages. Every marriage under heaven today is patterned after one of the two first families.

The First Original Family:

What Is Marriage?

Adam and Eve were the first original family. This family arrangement was perfect before the fall of man. The marriage also fell with the fall. The chances of the seed of families patterned after this first type of marriage becoming successful is half or 50:50 (i.e. Cain and Abel). This first type of family degenerated with time quickly into murder at the second generation and then into polygamy just at the fourth generation after Adam.

"And Lamech took unto him two wives: the name of the one was Adah, and the name of the other Zillah." (Gen.4:19)

Before long, this family also degenerated into homosexuality and lesbianism also referred to as Sodomy. Most marriages today are patterned after this first type of marriage.

The Second Original Family:
Jesus Christ and the Church are the second original family. The chance of failure of the seed of families under the second Adam is ratio one to twelve (1:12) i.e. the twelve disciples, only one turned out wayward. The rule under this second type of marriage is sacrificial love and

Every Marriage Can Work

submission as opposed to selfishness and exploitation under the first type of family.

Christian families should be patterned after the second original marriage. Every Christian family is supposed to be patterned after the example of the family arrangement between Christ and the Church. That is why the husband is commanded to love his wife just as Christ loves the Church and the wife is commanded to submit to her own husband just as the Church submits to Christ in the New Testament order.

The first original marriage is patterned after human traditions while the second marriage is patterned after the word of God. It is funny when a Christian couple chooses to pattern their marriage after human traditions. Such marriages don't work well. Most human traditions are embedded in the principles of selfishness, exploitation, superstition and oppression. A marriage sincerely and faithfully patterned after the word of God will work well and reflect the picture of heaven on earth.

CHAPTER TWO

God's Purpose For Marriage

God has a purpose for everything He made or created. According to Dr. Myles Munroe; *'when purpose is not known, abuse is inevitable'.* God has a purpose for the marriage institution. God formed marriage to meet certain needs and fulfil specific purposes. God's divine purpose for marriage can be summarized into three main objectives:

(1) Marriage is for Fellowship

"And the Lord God said, it is not good that the man should be alone; I will make him an help meet for him......... And the Lord God cause a deep sleep to fall

Every Marriage Can Work

upon Adam, and he slept and he took one of his ribs, and closed up the flesh instead thereof; And the rib, which the Lord God had taken from man, made he woman, and brought her unto the man. And Adam said, this is now bone of my bones, and flesh of my flesh; she shall be called woman, because she was taken out of man. Therefore shall a man leave his father and his mother, and shall cleave unto his wife: and they shall be one flesh. And they were both naked, the man and his wife, and were not ashamed."
(Gen.2:18, 20-25)

The first reason why God created the woman is for fellowship. Among all the animals God created, there was not found any creature that could fellowship with Adam. There was no suitable helper found for Adam. He was all alone in the garden. God saw Adam's loneliness and considered it as not good. So, God decided to help him. God did not create Eve in a hurry. God allowed Adam to feel the need for a companion first before creating the woman. God made the woman out of Adam's ribs. Adam had to let go of one of his ribs in order to have his treasured companion.

God's Purpose For Marriage

Adam was excited on sighting the woman. He exclaimed *"this is now bone of my bones and flesh of my flesh: she shall be called woman"* What Adam said could be interpreted to mean *"Yes! This is the kind of a companion I had been searching for! She is from me. She looks just like me! She shall be called woman."*

From the day Adam received Eve and got married to her, loneliness was curbed in his life. He now had somebody with whom they can care for each other and that can help him in the assignment that the Lord God gave to him to do.

Marriage is primarily for fellowship and for companionship. *"And they were naked, the man and his wife: and were not ashamed"*. Nakedness means they could share everything they have in common without feeling ashamed. They could share their minds and bodies. They are now one. Adam cleaved to his wife and they became one flesh. Therefore a man shall leave his parents and cleave to his wife so that they can become one flesh. Before a 'cleaving' to become one flesh, there must be a 'leaving' first. A man who needs to first run to his father or his mother to take instructions before doing anything together with his wife is yet to 'leave'. Such a man can

Every Marriage Can Work

never "cleave" to his wife unless he 'leaves' his father and mother.

Husbands and wives should not deny themselves quality time for fellowship. A woman was created primarily as a "fellowship-partner". That is why a woman cannot really do without talking and sharing quality time with her husband. It's either she has it or she is frustrated in the marriage. The man on the other hand, had been a keeper of the garden before he had the miracle of a companion. He still tends today, towards his job to the detriment of his God-given companion. A man's self esteem is built on his accomplishments while a woman's self esteem is built on relationships and appreciation. It takes the wisdom of God for a man to discern when his job is infringing on his marital commitments to his wife. The home comes first. Marriage should not be sacrificed on the altar of a job. Rather, a job could be sacrificed if need be, to keep the home together.

(2) Marriage is for procreation

"And God blessed them, and God said unto them, be fruitful and multiply, and replenish the earth, and subdue it....." (Gen.1:28)

God's Purpose For Marriage

The second purpose of marriage is for procreation. God blessed them and said: "Be fruitful and multiply". Marriage is the only platform ordained by God for procreation to take place. Having children out of wedlock is not God's will. It is not a part of the original purpose of God for the home.

The family is the most appropriate and conducive environment ordained by God for children to be born, nurtured and trained so that they can grow up to fulfil God's purpose in their lives. That is why when a home breaks, the children are also broken. Most juvenile delinquents are from broken homes, or were brought up outside marriage.

Fruitfulness is God's blessings upon the family. *"Be fruitful and multiply"* are two phrases joined by the conjunction 'and'. It can also be written as, "Be fruitful, be multiplied". God spoke these words into the lives of Adam and Eve the same way He said: *"let there be light"* in Gen.1:3. It is the same word of faith. When God said: *"let there be light"*, there was light. So, when God said: "be fruitful and multiply", the power "to be" entered Adam

Every Marriage Can Work

and Eve and empowered them for fruitfulness and multiplication.

A revelation of these words can deliver fruit of the womb to any marriage. Every marriage has been empowered by the eternal word of God for fruitfulness and multiplication. Since these words went forth, they had never been recalled by God. These words are still effective and powerful, accomplishing the purposes for which they were sent forth in the lives of men and women.

(3) Marriage is for effective dominion

"And God said, let us make man in our image, after our likeness and let them have dominion over the fish of the sea, and over the fowl of the air, and over the cattle, and over all the earth, and over every creeping thing that creepeth upon the earth.
So God created man in his own image, in the image of God created He him; male and female created He them. And God blessed them, and God said unto them, be fruitful, and multiply, and replenish the earth, and subdue it: and have dominion over the fish of the sea,

God's Purpose For Marriage

and over the fowl of the air, and over every living thing that moveth upon the earth." (Gen. 1:26-28)

The third purpose of marriage is for effective dominion over every other thing that God created. The woman is a help suitable and appropriate for the man to effectively fulfil God's purpose together with him.

It should be noted however that God said: *"...let them have dominion over..."*. This means that the man and the woman are to exercise dominion over every other creature of God together. The woman is not part of what the man is to dominate. Instead, the man and the woman are to come together as one to dominate other creatures of God.

In verse 28, the Bible says: "And God blessed them". God blessed the man and the woman together. A man cannot really enjoy God's blessings to the fullest alone. A woman cannot also enjoy God's blessings to the fullest alone. The blessing is for 'them', not for 'him' or 'her'.

Marriage is a divine laid out platform for companionship and fruitfulness. With marriage, it's a lot easier to replenish and subdue the earth. God has a purpose for

Every Marriage Can Work

everything he started. Marriage is designed to create the right atmosphere for a man and a woman to live together under the will of God.

CHAPTER TWO

Satan On The Attack

"For we wrestle not against flesh and blood, but against principalities, against powers, against rulers of the darkness of this world, against spiritual wickedness in high places." (Eph. 6:12)

Satan is our ultimate enemy. He is the archenemy of the people of God. We should not be ignorant of his devices. The devil is searching every day, using every available means to wage war against the family. The easiest way the devil can disintegrate the society is by attacking the family setup and pulling it down.

"For the weapon of our warfare are not carnal, but mighty through God to the pulling down of

Every Marriage Can Work

strongholds; casting down imaginations and every high thing that exalteth itself against the knowledge of God, and bringing into captivity every thought to the obedience of Christ." (II Cor. 10:4-5)

We have weapons of warfare in Christ, with which we can pull down any stronghold of the enemy, frustrating his plans and casting down every satanic imagination against our lives and homes.

There are various reasons why the devil is attacking the home so viciously, especially in this end time. Some of these reasons are:

(1) The synergic principle

Marriage provides a good platform for the synergic principle to operate. Satan cannot bear the effect of this fact, so he attacks the unity in the family.

Synergy is defined as the combined effect of forces that exceed the sum of individual efforts. For example, *"One chase a thousand and two put ten thousand to flight" (Deut. 32:30)*. If one will chase one thousand, then mathematically, two are supposed to chase two thousand.

Satan On The Attack

But what do we have? Two coming together are now chasing ten thousand! The effect of the force produced by their combination by far exceeds the sum of their individual efforts. This is called a synergic force or synergic principle.

Husbands and wives have the potential of doing much more together than the sum of what they can individually do or achieve. Satan is always threatened by this principle in marriage. He is always at peace when husband and wife can't see eye to eye. To do otherwise is to put the devil into trouble! I wish all Christian couples will have this understanding that it is the devil at work in their homes when there is no unity and peace among them. Couples should do everything possible to resolve their conflicts, be in unity and peace, so that the devil can always be in trouble!

Instead of husband and wife coming together to chase ten thousand, Satan wants them to chase only a maximum of one thousand individually and separately so that at the end, they would not have achieved more than twenty percent (20%) of their combined potentials. It is not possible for a man and a woman to attain their maximum

Every Marriage Can Work

potentials together as husband and wife when each partner is on his/her own. Couples should be wiser than this old trickster and liar called the devil. Couples should refuse to dance to the tune of the enemy of their marriage. They should find out what the word of God says about how to relate with each other and do it! Husband and wife should resolve to always put the devil to shame in their home.

(2) The Power of Agreement

"Again I say unto you, that if two of you shall agree on earth as touching any thing that they shall ask, it shall be done for them of my father which is in heaven." (Matt. 18:19)

"Can two walk together, except they be agreed?" (Amos 3:3)

Another thing the devil fears greatly in marriage is the power of agreement it provides. Satan also knows the scriptures. He knows that if two people, especially married people, shall agree together as touching anything in prayer, it shall be done. God is bound to do a thing, especially if it is influenced by the power of the agreement

Satan On The Attack

of two (minimum number needed for agreement). Satan can't bear the effect, when prayers prayed by couples are answered. So, he brings disagreement in between them. When couples disagree, they can't pray effectively together. Many couples don't even pray at all as a result of constant disagreements.

(3) The devil is a thief

"The thief cometh not, but for to steal, and to kill, and to destroy: I am come that they might have life, and that they might have it more abundantly." (John 10:10)

The ministry of the devil is stealing, killing and destroying. Jesus came to nullify Satan's ministry by giving life more abundantly.

"...For this purpose the Son of God was manifested, that He might destroy the works of the devil." (I John 3:8)

The thief likes to steal marital joy, kill the relationship and destroy the marriage. The devil uses various means

Every Marriage Can Work

to carry out his ministry against the home. He is fighting tooth and nail to make sure every marriage is destroyed. Satan has found good instruments in music, films, novels and the internet in these last days to wage real war against the foundation of the home.

Jesus Christ came that you may have life more abundantly and also that your marriage may have life! Just stay connected to the source of eternal life. Abundant life shall flow into your life and marriage ceaselessly. The ministry of the thief shall be frustrated in your life and home in Jesus name.

(4) The seed of the righteous

"Praise ye the Lord. Blessed is the man that feareth the Lord, that delighted greatly in his commandments. His seed shall be mighty upon the earth: the generation of the upright shall be blessed. Wealth and riches shall be in his house and his righteousness endureth forever"
(Psalm 112:1-3)

Satan is afraid of the seed of the righteous. He knows what the Bible says about the seed of the righteous. So,

Satan On The Attack

he wants to scatter the family so that those seeds of the righteous would not be able to grow to be mighty.

The children are the worst hit in a situation of a broken home. That is what the devil really wants to happen. He is after the seed of the righteous. It is not possible to fully comprehend the potentials of a seed. Inside a seed is a tree (potentially) that can bear fruits with seeds in them. Inside a seed is a potential forest! When the devil succeeds in destroying just one seed of the righteous, potential generations of the righteous are also destroyed with the seed.

We are not ignorant of the devices of the enemy. If the devil is whispering to your ears to call it quit, don't listen to him. He is targeting the future of your children. He wants to destroy the comfort that a united home provides for the children to grow to become mighty. Broken homes contribute the highest percentage of juvenile delinquents into the society. Parents have a divine responsibility towards their children. Don't let Satan scatter your home. Guide the future of your seeds jealously. You might be raising the future president of your country in your home now. You cannot possibly tell what any child can become

Every Marriage Can Work

in the future. They need the nest of your home and an environment filled with love to grow the way God ordained them to grow.

Some of the weapons Satan use to attack the family:

1. Ignorance:
"They know not, neither will they understand; they walk on in darkness: all the foundations of the earth are out of course." (Psalm 82:5)

Ignorance is a major weapon of the devil against a Christian. Satan knows that the moment you know the truth, your freedom is guaranteed. Satan has no new tricks. He keeps recycling the same tricks in all the areas of a Christian's life, shaded in different colours.

Lack of knowledge makes a man void of understanding. Lack of understanding causes a man to walk in the dark. In the dark, you cannot really see. You can't make real progress. You are bound to hit your feet against so many obstacles. Satan likes to keep a Christian perpetually in the dark until all the foundations (of the marriage) are out of course and the building eventually collapses.

Satan On The Attack

Every house is built by someone. Successful marriages don't just happen. They are made to happen. The knowledge of how to build a house is necessary if a house is going to be built successfully. The only antidote of ignorance is relevant education. The marriage institution is a school where the students never graduate until death separates, except they become rusticated and kicked out. For a successful home to be built there must be consistent learning. Ignorance can be killed through attending seminars, reading books or by simply asking questions.

Don't assume you know so much when it is evident in your marriage that you know so little. Humble yourself so that God can lift you up. Subject yourself to learning and be ready to make adjustments. That is how to build a great home.

2. Selfishness or self-centeredness
Another weapon of the devil against the family is the deadly weapon of self-centeredness. Selfishness is the direct opposite of love because the true meaning of love is 'giving'.

Every Marriage Can Work

A selfish husband cares not for how his wife feels. As long as he is alright, everybody should be alright. Selfishness destroys the home. Love is the cement that holds relationships together. Relationships easily fall apart where real love is lacking.

Once the devil can succeed in making one partner selfish, the relationship is as good as destroyed. The whole burden to love will tilt to one side and soon, the overburdened partner gets tired and ready to give up.

Selfishness is not a fruit of the spirit, but love is. Satan is behind the spirit of selfishness and self-centeredness. Don't let him take you over. God's will is for you to have a prosperous family life.

3. Unforgiveness
Marriage is a blending of two people with different backgrounds, experiences and natural makeup. There is bound to be conflicts along the line as the blending progresses. No marriage can survive without the forgiving spirit. If you've gotten to a point in your relationship where forgiveness is no longer possible, Satan is definitely at work one way or the other.

Satan On The Attack

If God could forgive you your trespasses, then you can forgive. Forgiveness really is releasing yourself from the chain you bound yourself with because of what somebody else did to you. Unforgiving attitude can compound into deadly diseases. Many killer diseases are as a result of emotional problems. Don't allow the devil to destroy your marriage and your health with the spirit of unforgiving. Learn to forgive. You can do it for Christ's sake!

4. Unfaithfulness

There is no satanic weapon that is as strong against the family as much as when a partner becomes unfaithful. The sin of adultery hits directly against the oneness of marriage. The lure to have extra marital affair is a subtle satanic attack against the family. The same Satan that lure a man to sin will also help the man to get exposed. Satan's work is only half done when he succeeds in luring a man to sin. To complete his job, he must make sure that the man reaps the consequences of his sins. It is God that does not wish that a sinner should perish but come to repentance. Satan wants every sinner to perish quickly before they can get the opportunity to repent.

Every Marriage Can Work

There is no reason good enough for unfaithfulness to occur in a marriage. Marriage is a life time commitment. Satan always comes in a subtle way.

"Abstain from all appearance of evil."
(I Thess. 5:22)

"Flee also youthful lusts: but follow righteousness."
(II Tim. 2:22)

Don't give in to temptation. Joseph was greatly tempted, but he stood his ground. Even though he went to jail for righteousness sake, he eventually became the prime minister of Egypt.

Sometimes, Satan can use your boss, especially if you are a lady. Your job might be threatened unless you agree to have an affair. You don't really need to spend time to think of what to do as a Christian. Choose your marriage and quit the job if need be. God will eventually take you to your palace.

It takes strong determination and the fear of God to overcome the temptation of having an affair and the momentary pleasures it offers. Don't allow Satan to

Satan On The Attack

wrestle your marriage away from you by luring you into unfaithfulness.

Fornication and adultery are also sins against God with severe divine punishments. Be wiser than the devil.

CHAPTER FOUR

Seven Reasons Why Every Marriage Can Work

Why are so many marriages not working? Is it true that they can't possibly work? There is no marriage that can't possibly work. It is possible. I believe that every marriage can work. This means that every marriage has the potential and ability to work if the partners are willing to learn and do those things that matter in making the marriage work. It is God's will for every marriage to be successful but, the final decision lies with every couple.

Every house is built by someone. This means that magnificent edifices don't accidentally occur. Somebody would have to pay the price, spend the time and sacrifice a lot of resources for the edifice to stand. The simple truth is that marriages don't work until couples are ready to make it work. Marriages don't work automatically as

Every Marriage Can Work

a result of the social status of couples. Marital failure is no respecter of status. Every marriage can work, but not every marriage will work. The reason why every marriage will not work is because every couple will not pay necessary attention to their marriage. If every couple would pay attention to their marriage and do things that will make their marriage to work, then every marriage will work excellently.

I believe the premise that "every marriage can work" is where to start from in finding solution to marital problems. If there is no faith in the possibility of marriages working, then there is no need finding solutions to marital problems. Of course, we know as a matter of fact that despite the bad statistics, some marriages are still working. If some marriages can work, then there is the possibility for every other marriage to work. Here are the seven reasons why I believe every marriage can work:

1. Marriage is God's design and idea

God is the designer and the manufacturer of the marriage institution. Marriage is not man's idea. Adam never knew anything about marriage until God conceptualized it and presented Eve to him. On sighting Eve, Adam's face glowed. He was full of excitement and declared: ***"This is now bone of my bones, and flesh of my flesh. She shall be called woman, because she was taken out of Man" (Gen. 2:23).*** Marriage was not a product of Adam's

Seven Reasons Why Every Marriage Can Work

thinking. It was a product of God's thinking. So, we can say marriage is God's product.

Everything God made was good, perfect and excellent. *"And God saw everything that he had made, and behold, it was very good" (Gen. 1:31).* If everything God created was very good, then marriage is good. The family institution is a super design of God. The product is excellent and perfect, but put into the hands of imperfect humans who make imperfect choices most of the time. To enjoy marriage, you must see the hand of God in it. You must accept the fact that God knows everything about marriage because He created it. If you see marriage as something that does not concern God, then you miss the whole point. Marriage is founded on God's wisdom and expertise. God is interested in every marriage and still acts as the umpire in marriage relationships (Mal 2:14).

If you want to maximally enjoy a product, get the manufacturer's instruction on how to operate the product by reading the user's manual. God's word is the user's manual that came with the product called marriage. No one can know a product as much as the one who puts it together. Using a product in disregard of the instructions in the users' manual can destroy the product. This is why any marriage that runs in contrary to divine principles in God's word will surely meet a brick wall. Amazingly, if those who don't believe in God can run their marriage

Every Marriage Can Work

according to God's principles, they will surely have a successful marriage.

We are going to use the analogy of a motor car, designed and manufactured by man to illustrate marriage as a design and product of God. Marriage did not happen to man by chance. It was created by God's intention. It was a deliberate thought of God. God had something in His mind for establishing the marriage institution. He designed it, manufactured it and made it available to man. Motor cars don't just appear in show rooms. Every motor car we see in the show room or on the road is a product of someone's thinking and design. A lot of processes go into the manufacturing before it is made available for use to a buyer. These cars moving on the road today are only working because the owners are following the manufacturer's instructions. None has been designed to keep on working when it's not maintained. With every new car, comes an owner's manual, so that the owner can know how to effectively use and care for it.

No matter how expensive and beautiful your car is, it cannot serve you well if you don't follow the designer's recommendations in the owner's manual. Sometimes, you may not fully grasp why a designer gives certain instructions in the user's manual. You really don't have to understand everything into details. You need not fully understand the mechanics of a motor car before you can

Seven Reasons Why Every Marriage Can Work

use one. You just follow the instructions and you will enjoy the product. For example, anybody can query why the designers of motor vehicles instruct that fuel be put into a big tank called fuel tank, while water is to be put into a smaller tank called the radiator. Anybody can think about it that since fuel is expensive, it should be put into the smaller tank (radiator) while water that is very cheap should be put into the bigger tank (fuel tank). That makes economical sense. Isn't it? It is evident that anyone who thinks like this is going to ground his car in no time. The car will not work with water in the fuel tank. The engine will just not start no matter how clean the water is. Simple instructions from manufacturers are to be followed in order to enjoy their products.

If God says: 'women submit to your husband', it means that is one of the things to do for a woman to enjoy her marriage. Going against this instruction will not make any marriage to work. God also says to the man to love his wife sacrificially. If a man is so full of himself and so selfish in relating with his wife, he cannot possibly enjoy his marriage.

Products need maintenance. No matter how beautiful a new car is, for the user to enjoy it for a long time, he must pay enough attention to maintaining the car. When fuel level is low, he must drive the car to a gas station for refill. If he is too busy and can't spare the time to do that,

Every Marriage Can Work

he may end up discovering how foolish he had been when the car stops in the middle of the road. Imagine a business man that is going for an important meeting with a near zero fuel in his car. If he is so busy and too much in a hurry to spend a little time to refill his tank, will he arrive on time for his 'important' appointment? Not really, as the car is bound to stop working as soon as the fuel level reaches zero. Married people also should not expect their marriage to keep running smoothly without any form of maintenance. This requires time, attention and resources. You need to frequently and regularly refill your relationship with the fuel of love. It is compulsory. You really don't have a choice if you want that relationship to get to its destination. To do otherwise is to ground it. It's amazing for car users to imagine they can keep driving a car when fuel level is zero!

As you keep using your vehicle which was designed by a fellow man, you need to service it periodically and replace worn-out or damaged parts. Every morning, you need to check the state of the engine by making sure that enough water is where water should be and that fuel and oil are also sufficient in the places they are supposed to be. If you assume to know more than the designer and you put water where oil should be, then the car will find it very difficult to serve you. It then starts malfunctioning. Everything must be put in its required place and in sufficient quantities for the car to work effectively. This

Seven Reasons Why Every Marriage Can Work

is exactly the same way marriage works. Every necessary thing that a marriage needs to have in order for it to work as designed must be known (by reading the manual) and put into place for the marriage to work effectively and smoothly as designed by God. As a user of a product, you can't have a superior idea to that of the manufacturer. You can't know a product better than the designer. Just follow simple instructions. That's how to be smart!

When you start off in the morning and you insert your key into the ignition, there is a certain sound you expect to hear as the engine starts. If you hear a different or an unpleasant sound, it shows that the car is malfunctioning. You don't throw the car away at this point and conclude it just can't work. What you do is to call in somebody who can fix the problem for you. When that is done, the car is surely on the road again. If you refuse to pay timely attention to your car, a little fault may degenerate into bigger problems. When a marriage starts making funny sounds, it also needs a check up. For example, by the time a couple starts greeting themselves through their noses, their marriage is already making a funny sound, because that is not the way a marriage should sound. Wise couples will attend to whatever the problem is, resolve it and move on. Foolish couples will ignore that funny sound and keep driving the relationship, not minding the funny

Every Marriage Can Work

sound. Eventually, what will happen is that the small problem is going to degenerate into a bigger one and may end up destroying other parts of that relationship. By the time they are forced to attend to the marriage, several other things would have been affected. So, if couples would run their marriages according to the instructions of the manufacturer (God), adequately maintain and service their relationship, their marriage will work. At times, you can keep flogging a malfunctioning car as long as it is moving. When this happens, you can be sure that the car will soon break down in the middle of the road and it's going to be very painful to you. Marriages don't have to break down before couples are 'forced' to attend to a malfunctioning relationship.

Why are so many marriages not working? We may as well ask the same question about human inventions that why are so many cars not working, grounded and jacked up. The answer is very simple and obvious. It is definitely not the fault of the manufacturer or the product. It is rather, the fault of the end user(s). No car is manufactured with the intention that shortly after the end user had paid a lot of money to own it, it will then become unworkable. If it malfunctions and the owner pays attention to it, it will start working well again. Every car manufactured and sold to a customer is designed to work. The same way,

Seven Reasons Why Every Marriage Can Work

marriage was not designed by God to end up in separation or divorce. In the beginning, it was not so. It is the hardness of men's heart that leads them to divorce, not the non-workability of the marriage institution. ***"He saith unto them, Moses because of the hardness of your hearts suffered you to put away your wives: but from the beginning it was not so" (Matt 19:18).*** God designed marriage to last for a lifetime.

Some vehicles had been grounded for many years. Many already have dusts settled on them, with cobwebs everywhere and rusted parts. Many had been thrown away and given up as junks. As factual as this is about many marriages, it is also true that if such vehicles or marriage relationships can be worked on, and given proper attention, it is just a matter of time; very soon, you will see the same vehicle working like any other vehicle on the road. No matter how bad a marriage relationship is, if the couple is willing and determined to pay attention to the marriage and spend time to develop intimacy, the marriage will take a new turn and start working.

This means there are no nonworking marriages, only malfunctioning marriages. There is no marriage that can't work if the appropriate things are done by the two people involved in the marriage. Malfunctioning marriages only show that those marriages need attention. It does not mean that the marriage should be grounded or thrown away.

Every Marriage Can Work

People don't throw their cars away at any slight malfunctioning. They pay quick attention to their cars. If your car malfunctions and you can't fix the problem, call in the technicians. The same way, if your marriage malfunctions and you can't fix the problem, seek for godly counsel and you will be surprised how easily the supposed big problem can be solved. A man's ignorance is his mountain. One day, my car had a fault and I tried to fix the problem, using trial and error methods for over two hours without any success. Eventually, I called in an auto technician who amazingly fixed the problem in less than five minutes. Trial and error methods can work sometimes, but at other times, it can be frustrating. If your marriage malfunctions, call in the 'technicians'. They will help you see your marriage in a way you've never seen it before and point out where you need to work on or change an approach. To the glory of God, I have seen couples who had separated for years having their marriages restored after attending some of our marriage seminars. There is no marital problem that cannot be solved if the willingness to solve the problem is there. If marriage principles are not worked out, a marriage cannot work. If you enter into a business partnership with a friend and afterwards, you do nothing, nothing will work. If you refuse to set up the office, the office cannot set up itself. You and your partner need to invest resources, time and energy into the business for profiting to come. Do I need to add that you must do it right? Business people spend time and resources

Seven Reasons Why Every Marriage Can Work

training and retraining just to be up to date and get things right. So is marriage. Your marriage can surely work only if you are ready to work it!

2. Love is like a spark of fire

We often hear the word 'fire' being used to describe 'love'. For example: "when the fire of their love was still burning ..." Yes, love is like a fire, but it starts as a spark. When a man meets a woman, there develops a spark of an emotional feeling or attraction. No matter how small this "spark" is it is potentially capable of leading to friendship and eventually, marriage if the emotional feelings are well nurtured from both ends. It therefore means that before a man and a woman can come together in marriage, there must have been a sort of an attraction or a good emotional feeling towards each other. Even those who didn't plan for marriage but were just friends and eventually something developed between them, the woman gets pregnant and they had to marry, had a spark of love or attraction that made them become friends in the first place.

There is something about sparks of fire. Any spark of fire is potentially, a big fire. A spark of a match stick can set a building on fire. The same spark of a match stick can simply be put out and soon forgotten as nothing. What any spark of fire needs to become a conflagration is a conducive environment for fire to grow. Such environment has to do with flammable materials and enough air. Any

Every Marriage Can Work

spark of fire that finds itself in the midst of fuel, surrounded by wood, clothing and other flammable materials will quickly grow into a big fire. At the beginning, it might be easier to put out a fire, but as soon as the fire gathers momentum, it becomes more difficult to be put out. By the time it becomes a conflagration; it goes on consuming everything on its path and cannot be easily put out any longer.

If love is like a spark of fire, it then follows that if that little attraction at the beginning of the relationship can be given the conducive environment to grow, it will become bigger and bigger until it becomes very difficult for any fire fighter or love-fighter in this case, to put out such love. The environment for love to grow basically has to do with what lovers say and do to each other. Affectionate words, words of commendation and appreciation are fuels and wood to the fire of love. Caring, sacrificial giving, helping each other, forgiving each other, praying for each other, speaking words seasoned with salt and going all out to make each other comfortable are necessary fuels and air needed for any spark of love to become a big fire of love that cannot be easily put out. On the contrary, words of insult, name calling, abusive words, battering, cheating on spouse and irresponsible living are fire fighters' water that can easily put out the fire in any love.

Seven Reasons Why Every Marriage Can Work

If couples can give their relationship the environment to grow, the spark of fire in their love will grow; become an all consuming flame and a passionate fire of love. On the contrary, if neither of them care nor have time to pay attention to their relationship, the relationship will soon die. The spark of fire will be put out and it will look as if the marriage couldn't have worked.

Apart from what couples say and do to each other, there are also some environments or circumstances that normally don't help love to grow. For example, couples that are still living under the same roof with their parents/in-laws have put their relationship at a disadvantage. The word of God says, ***"Therefore shall a man leave his father and his mother and shall cleave unto his wife and they shall be one flesh" (Gen. 2:2:24)***. A break of this divine principle puts the marriage at the mercy of the parents/in-laws. Things cannot just go right the way it should. Another circumstance that a marriage can be subjected to that can easily and quickly put out the fire of love is when husband and wife are not living together. Some couples live in two different countries and still assume they are married until real life situations prove them wrong. There must be a 'cleaving' which means a continual physical contact for any marriage to run smoothly and successfully. Of course, living together on its own does not determine the success of a relationship,

Every Marriage Can Work

but it is one of the prerequisites to having a successful marriage.

Every marriage can work if instead of pouring water on the fire of love; couples are fanning up the flame of their love with positive actions, positive words and creating conducive environment. We all know by experience that every couple will not take these positive steps to grow their love because growing love takes sacrifice and hard work. That is why so many marriages are not working. If any couple can come to this consciousness today, make a lot of adjustments and start doing things right in their relationship, the fire of love in that marriage will pick up and start to grow. So, it is possible for any marriage to work if couples will learn the right things, change their approach and start doing things right. Is your love growing and the fire burning? Keep fanning it and increasing the fire. Is the fire of your relationship out? You can still fan the embers to flame and recover lost grounds. It is possible. You can do it!

3. The first marriage has greater advantages.
There is no other marriage like the first one. So many people with experience can attest to this. When two youthful hearts melt into one, it is a miracle. Getting married is supposed to be for young people. It was not primarily designed for those who already have all the experience. People can remarry at any age if they have

Seven Reasons Why Every Marriage Can Work

to, but such marriages cannot be compared to the tenderness of two youthful hearts beating as one. Except in very few exceptional cases, the first marriage is usually the best.

Many who left their first marriage to get into the second, third or fourth marriage eventually come to find out that the first marriage has greater advantages over every other subsequent marriage. In the first marriage, there is no basis for comparison. It is just the husband and the wife. In second marriages, there is a basis for comparison. The woman may eventually conclude that the first man was better off after all, or that all men are the same! A man in a second marriage may also eventually find out that what he thought he hated in the first woman is even more conspicuous in the second woman. For example, a man once confided in me that he was going to divorce his wife because she talks too much. He didn't realize that all women talk. If he had married another woman because of this reason, he would have been more frustrated. There is nothing any man can do about feminine gender traits. They are there present in every woman. There is nothing any woman can also do about masculine gender traits. They are there present in every man. The gender traits are what make men to be men and women to be women. Another man complained that his wife does not think like him. He did not know this is a normal situation for men and women to think differently on a lot of issues.

Every Marriage Can Work

There is this biblical example of a beloved Samaritan woman who wanted a perfect marriage with a perfect man. When Jesus asked her to go and call her husband, she told Jesus that she was a single lady. Jesus replied her that she was right by saying she had no husband because she already had five and was living with the sixth man who was not her husband.

"... Thou hast well said, I have no husband: For thou hast had five husbands; and he whom thou now hast is not thy husband: in that saidst thou truly" (John 4:17-18)

This woman actually thought in her heart that Jesus was a possible suitor. The question is: what actually was she looking for in all those men that she has not found? The grass is always greener on the other side (until you get there!). This saying is very true in marriage relationship. Jesus eventually made her realize that the solution to her marital problems was a change in her, not a consistent change of men. Except for the death of a spouse, if every man and woman will take care of their first marriage, there will be no need for a second or third or fourth! Every marriage can work because the first marriage is still the best. Are you thinking of moving in with another man? The guy looks 'greener' than your present husband. It's just a deceit of the devil. Someone who broke up with his ex and is now very nice to you will also break up

Seven Reasons Why Every Marriage Can Work

with you, leaving you in the cold with a lot of regrets. Don't fall for the lure. There's nothing to it. Work on your marriage. Your present marriage is better than the next, eventually.

4. Those who divorce and those who stay married had basically the same kind of problems.
There are no new marital problems. Name it, and I will tell you it has happened before. Name the problem and I will tell you or even show you so many other couples in the same boat with you. Nothing is really new under heaven!

There are so many reasons why couples divorce. Tell me why a couple had to divorce and I will search out in that same community, at least, one other couple who are in the same situation and are still married. Conflicts are not the problems in a marriage, but **unresolved conflicts**. When conflicts are not resolved, it leads to more and more conflicts until the center can no longer hold. It has been discovered that the basic issues that lead to divorce in so many marriages are also present in the marriages of those who opt to stay married. The guy who told me he was going to divorce his wife because she talks too much was shocked when I informed him that my wife talks too! Nothing is new under heaven.

Every Marriage Can Work

To stay married is a choice. To divorce is also a choice. The choice to divorce is different from the challenges or problems on ground. No matter how bad a situation is, a couple still has the opportunity to decide for or against their marriage relationship. Our decisions are generally informed by the information that is available to us. If a couple can have the knowledge that their differences are meant to complement each other, they will not allow their differences to scatter them. Every marriage has the potential to work. Therefore, every marriage can work if every couple can see their marriage in a better light and allow their love to win in every situation.

5. Divorce creates a bigger problem than it pretends to solve.
Many see divorce as a solution to their marital problems. Divorce is not a solution. It may give a temporary relieve, but the divorce situation eventually leads to more problems than it pretends to have solved.

The more times a person remarries, the more difficult it becomes for that individual to stay married. From research works, divorce rate in first marriages is said to be 40%, while in second marriages, divorce rate is 60%. In third marriages, divorce rate is 75%! The more number of marriages, the slimmer the chances of enjoying a successful marriage.

Seven Reasons Why Every Marriage Can Work

There can't be a smooth divorce. Divorce necessary has to be a tearing apart. Individual partners are not completely whole after a divorce. A part of them is in the other partner and a part of the other partner is in them for life.

Divorce does not stop couples from seeing each other again especially if there are children in the union. Each time they see at their child's graduation, wedding or other ceremonies, they relive the pains of the past. Everybody will be happy at the occasion except the two of them once they sight each other.

The new partner in a new marriage also stands the chance of being made to pay for the errors of the former partner. This on its own is a keg of gun powder, waiting to explode into conflicts very soon. Each partner wants to be very careful and defensive of their emotions. Once beaten, twice shy. This kind of situation does not help a healthy relationship to form.

This is not to say that there are no situations where divorce or separation can be recommended. In situations where there is a visible threat to life, it is not advisable to remain in that kind of relationship. A man once went nuts and threatened to kill his wife. The wife ran to her parents who asked her to return to her husband. They assumed the man did not mean what he said. Eventually the man

Every Marriage Can Work

killed his wife and her parents regretted their actions. Couples need to stay alive to be married. A marriage covenant terminates at the death of a spouse. It takes two to agree. So, couples may be advised to excuse themselves if their relationship is taking a dangerous dimension. Nevertheless, divorce is not a solution to marital problems. The solution to marital problems is for couples to sit down, evaluate their relationship and fashion out ways to resolve their conflicts amicably, turn a new leaf, improve on their communication and change their approach to their marriage.

Instead of couples to always think of divorce in solving their marital problems, they should rather think of how to resolve their conflicts. Divorce should not even be mentioned under any circumstance in a healthy marriage.

6. There is no perfect, flawless and faultless partner

They say love is blind, but marriage is the eye opener. There is no way a couple can fully know each other while courting. During courtship, partners present their best side. After marriage, the other side can now be fully seen.

There is no perfect, flawless and faultless partner. You may see a couple from afar and think everything is perfect about them. It's when you move closer to them that you see that they have their own times of misunderstanding and challenges too.

Seven Reasons Why Every Marriage Can Work

A successful marriage is not a marriage between two perfect, flawless and faultless partners. It is rather, a relationship between two people who are determined to work on their imperfections, flaws and faults. So, when you experience the flaws in your partner, that is not the time to call it quit. Your partner's flaws are a reflection of your own flaws too. Focus on the strength of your partner, not his weaknesses. We are all made of strength and weaknesses. We don't rush into marriage. You must know the strength and weaknesses of your partner to an extent before going into marriage. Once you make up your mind to go into that marriage relationship, do your best to stay true to your decision.

7. There is no individual without virtues

It takes two to fight. It also takes two to tango. There is no man or woman that is made of all flaws and imperfections. There is no individual without virtues. The problem is that couples don't focus on the virtues in their partners. They'll rather focus on the flaws.

If couples can start seeing the virtues in their partners, it will be easier to overlook the faults. At least, something attracted them to each other at the beginning of their relationship. They should focus on those virtues and good things while working to improve on their areas of imperfections.

Every Marriage Can Work

In conclusion, a successful marriage requires hard work. Those who have a successful marriage today worked on their relationship. If every couple can work hard on their relationship, their marriage will work.

CHAPTER FIVE

What Helps marriage To Work

There are two relational dimensions that help marriage to work. If these two dimensions are intact, then every marriage can work. These two relational dimensions are:

***1. The individual partner's relationship with God
and
2. The relationship between the husband and wife.***

These relationships can be illustrated with a relational triangle.

Every Marriage Can Work

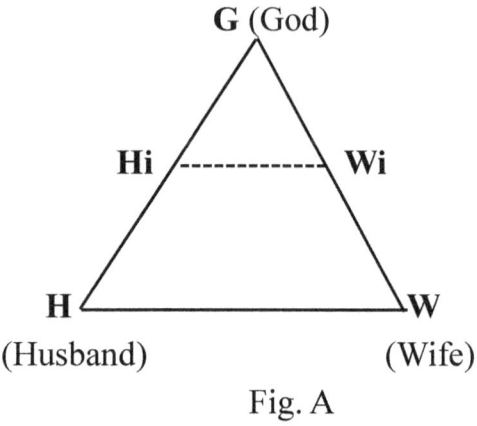

Fig. A

From the above triangle, line HG stands for the relationship between the husband and God while line WG represents the relationship between the wife and God.

Line HW however represents the relationship between the husband and his wife. This triangle gives us a threefold cord that is not quickly broken.

"Two are better than one... if they fall, the one will lift up his fellow......And if one prevail against him, two shall withstand him, and a threefold cord is not quickly broken."   *(Eccl. 4:12)*

What Helps Marriage To Work

The three lines of the triangle must be connected as shown in the triangle to form a perfect triangular shape. If one line is missing as in figure B and C below, it shows that the marriage relationship is not complete.

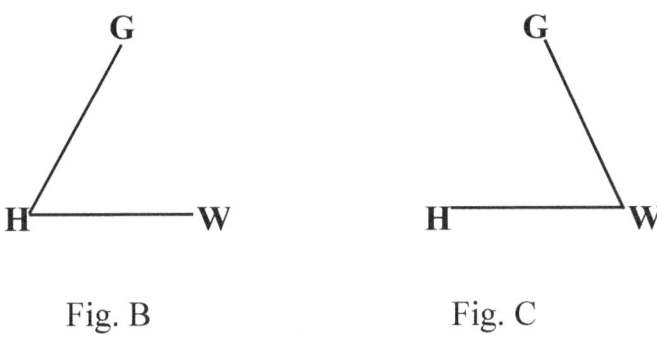

Fig. B   Fig. C

What really helps marriages to be perfectly bounded together is the complete triangular structure of the relationship. In Fig. A, as husband and wife get more intimately related to God, they also get more and more intimately related to each other. This is illustrated by the shorter distance between the points in triangle Hi, G, Wi as compared to triangle HG, WG, HW.

The individual partner's relationship with God
The individual partner should maintain a cordial and growing relationship with God. The individual's

Every Marriage Can Work

relationship with God already takes care of so many problems that can easily tear a marriage apart. A man who maintains a growing and intimate relationship with God will not be a liar, an adulterer or somebody given to wrath. He won't be a drunkard or a wife-abuser. He won't be given to drugs, smoking or pornography.

Researches had shown that Christian families have better chances of surviving than non-Christian ones. The fear of God, the ability to love with the love of God, the word of God and humility all help a marriage to endure the storms of life. Kay Arthur wrote in her book *"A Marriage Without Regrets"* about what glues a man and a woman together in marriage:

"It is the glue of maintaining an intimate, surrendered relationship with our father, of determining that God and His word will have priority over self that actually helps a man and a woman to stick together." [1]

Relationship between Husband and Wife
Next to the individual's relationship with God is the relationship between the husband and the wife. How husband and wife relate goes a long way in determining whether the marriage will work or not.

What Helps Marriage To Work

The marriage relationship comes first before every other human relationship. The home is to be given a priority over job, business, ministry, friends or the extended family. In introducing Deborah, the woman of God, the relationships in her life were written in the order of priority.

"And Deborah, a prophetess, the wife of Lapidoth, she judged Israel at that time." (Judges 4:4)

The introduction starts with Deborah as a person, followed by her relationship with God. She was a prophetess of God. The next priority to her relationship with God is her relationship with her husband. She was the wife of Lapidoth. Next to her marital relationship and responsibilities is her ministry. She was a judge in Israel.

The scripture already showed us how things should be arranged in order of priority in our lives through the example of the introduction of Deborah. As a judge, Deborah had a very busy schedule, but that never took the place of her responsibilities at home. At home, she was a wife and a mother. Any man who places his marriage as secondary to his job, business or ministry will definitely have a difficult marriage.

Every Marriage Can Work

The same thing goes for a woman who does not know how her children are growing up as a result of busy schedules at work or business. No matter how busy a man or a woman's job might be, if the home is given a priority, time will always be created to spend with the family. The order of priority in relationships should be the man, his relationship with God, his family, his ministry/vocation and others.

The relationship between the husband and wife should be regularly worked at. There can always be improvements. Learn what love means to your spouse. Discover how your spouse wishes to be loved and start working at loving him/her every day. Learn to speak your spouse's love language. Do everything you can to improve your relationship with your wife or your husband.

These two dimensions of relationship are very much needed to be in proper place for a marriage relationship to work effectively. These dimensions of relationship help husband and wife to be glued together so much that nothing but death can separate them.

CHAPTER SIX

Consequences Of A Dysfunctional Marriage

What happens when things go bad in a marriage? Since humans are interdependent on one another, the ripple effect of a bad marriage goes beyond the husband and the wife that are involved. All couples have a responsibility from God to maintain a peaceful and responsible family life for overall peace to reign in the society.

A. Consequences on couples

1. Emotional disturbances
Couples who are having turbulent marriages also suffer a lot of emotional disturbances. Top on the list of what

Every Marriage Can Work

commonly triggers emotional disorder is love-failure or lack of love and acceptance. Other things like bad finance and tragedies can also cause emotional imbalance, but a stable love life stabilizes emotions naturally.

2. Poor health

Most health problems stem from emotional problems. Depression easily sets in when there is a failed love-life. Most killer diseases like hypertension, high blood pressure, etc., are usually triggered by emotional problems. Poor marriages lead to poor health.

3. Poor human relations

Couples in dysfunctional marriages also usually have bad relationships with other people. They sometimes take out their marital frustrations on others around them. It's either they become excessively nice to prove they are not as wicked as portrayed by their partners, or they become too difficult on people around them.

A fulfilling marriage enhances a good and balanced interpersonal relationship with people outside the marriage.

Consequences Of A Dysfunctional Marriage

4. Mental illness
A failed love life can also lead to mental illness. Many people in mental hospitals today would not have been there only if they had a successful marriage.

B. Consequences on children

1. Defective emotional growth
Children raised in unhealthy marriages usually develop defective emotional growth. The love life of a father and mother affects the emotional growth of their children. Many children grow up living in fear of everything because fear was the only language the father knew how to speak. A home that is usually full of tension will produce children that are always on edge.

2. Rebellion
Children usually resort to rebellion when they feel it's time they react to the injustice in their family. When there is no love and warmness in the family, potentially rebellious children are being nurtured.

3. Bad future relationships

Every Marriage Can Work

Since children see their parents as role models, it is not unusual to see a grown up child repeating the errors of his/her parents. A girl who grew under an abusive father will assume all men are like her father. This will negatively affect the way she is going to relate to her husband. A boy who grew up seeing his mother's men-friends will easily suspect his wife for any reason. Love cannot thrive in an atmosphere of suspicion.

C. Consequences on the society

1. *Increase in domestic violence*
Dysfunctional marriages usually lead to domestic violence. This negatively impacts the society. Increase in domestic violence gives the society a bad image at home and abroad. It stresses security personnel who also have to cope with criminals on the streets.

2. *Increase in rate of divorce*
Dysfunctional marriage can end up in a divorce if not quickly attended to. Increase in rate of divorce in a society shows that the society is gradually breaking down and disintegrating. Something quickly needs to be done even

Consequences Of A Dysfunctional Marriage

by world governments to promote family health in our societies.

3. Juvenile delinquency
Broken homes are the nurseries for juvenile delinquents. Delinquent children easily grow up to be full-time criminals except they encounter a change of heart on the way.

D. Harmonious family life is possible
The consequences of a bad marriage are so grave that every couple need to sit up and fashion out ways to live harmoniously with their partners. Most times, it takes more energy to fight than to live harmoniously together. Couples should channel their energies to work together towards having and maintaining a harmonious family life.

What it takes to have a successful family life is a decision. If a man or a woman can take a decision and follow the decision with determination and commitment, virtually anything is possible to achieve on earth. You can read more about the principle of decision and commitment in the concluding chapter.

CHAPTER SEVEN

Conflict Resolution

Conflict within a marriage context occurs when there are disagreements, arguments or quarrels. As husband and wife learn to blend together, there is bound to be times of disagreements, arguments and quarrels. It is not possible for husband and wife never to have had conflicts in their relationship. Marriage is a coming together of two people who had been raised from two different and distinct backgrounds. It is practically impossible never to have opposing views on issues occasionally.

Husbands and wives do hurt themselves. Many times, not intentionally, but a spouse's action can translate into a hurtful experience to his/her partner without actually

Every Marriage Can Work

intending to hurt his/her feelings. For example, while having a little argument, the husband might raise his voice and the wife coils in, feeling hurt for being shouted upon. If this kind of a small and very simple conflict is not resolved, it might aggravate into something very big and eventually very difficult to handle.

Husbands and wives need to learn how to resolve their conflicts amicably and quickly. The Bible talked about the importance of conflict resolution and forgiveness:

"Be ye angry and sin not. Let not the sun go down upon your wrath."
   (Eph. 4:26)

"Therefore, if thou bring thy gift to the altar, and there rememberest that thy brother hath ought against thee, leave there thy gift before the altar, and go thy way, first be reconciled to thy brother, and then come and offer thy gift."   *(Matt. 5:23)*

"Then came Peter to him, and said, how oft shall my brother sin against me, and I forgive him till seven

Conflict Resolution

times? Jesus saith unto him, I say not unto thee until seven times but, until seventy times seven."
    (Matt. 18:21-22)

Not allowing the sun to go down on your anger means you must not allow a conflict to roll over into the next day. Conflicts must be resolved the same day. Even if you remember you have an unresolved conflict while offering a sacrifice to God in the temple, Jesus recommended you suspend the worship and first go and resolve the conflict. How many husbands and wives go to church today to sing praises to God and give offerings while they are almost no longer talking to each other?

Building trust
Trust is one of the pillars of marriage. The opposite of trust is suspicion. To trust your spouse is to believe in the honesty and worth of your spouse. No marriage can really thrive under the atmosphere of suspicion.

Trust can be built through consistent behaviour in different circumstances that shows your mate that you can be trusted. If you are somebody who finds it difficult to keep

Every Marriage Can Work

your words, then, it's going to be very hard for your spouse to trust you.

Trust is needed in conflict resolution. Your spouse must be able to trust or believe in the sincerity of your words and actions. Let your spouse see consistently that you are a man or a woman of integrity. This will help you to be able to easily resolve your conflicts.

Benefit of a doubt
In resolving conflicts, always give your spouse, the benefit of doubt. Assume in all cases the sincerity and innocence of your spouse until you listen to his/her explanations. No man is perfect though; always believe that your husband or wife could not have intentionally decided to hurt you. Don't judge your marriage partner before you hear his/her own side of the story.

If it matters to your spouse, it matters
Many times, conflicts are never resolved because one partner feels a complaint is a flimsy matter. If anything matters to your spouse, then accept that it matters. If an issue that looks trivial to you is disturbing your spouse, then you should also feel disturbed by it. Never treat any complain from your spouse as trivial or an *"it doesn't*

Conflict Resolution

matter" issue. Some things that matter to men don't matter seriously to women while some things that matter to women don't matter that much to men. In conflict resolution, you must have it as a rule at the back of your mind that if something matters to your spouse, then it matters.

Don't give in to anger
While in a conflict, never give in to anger. Never allow anger to take over your emotions and senses. Never lose charge of yourself. Curtailing your anger in the midst of crisis is the first step towards conflict resolution. The more control of yourself you lose to anger, the more difficult and tedious it becomes to resolve the conflict. You may be rightly angry, but don't go beyond the level of merely being angry into sinning. Anytime you are almost losing control to anger, apply the brake of self-control.

Discuss the conflict
Discuss the conflict as soon as possible. If you were offended by your spouse, tell him/her in a plain and clear language, what happened and how you got offended. Stick to the point of discourse. Don't draw analogies from

Every Marriage Can Work

several other resolved instances in the past. State your mind with a view to finding out what really happened from your spouse's point of view. Curtail your emotions and lower your voice when confronting your spouse. Don't insult or abuse. Confront for a resolution of the conflict, not just to make a point. Confront with love, giving your spouse the benefit of a doubt.

Learn to say: "I am sorry"
If an issue matters to your spouse, then it matters. Never waive off your spouse's hurt as insignificant nor describe it as childish. If something bothers your spouse, then allow that same thing to bother you.

Listen to your spouse. Allow your spouse to finish expressing himself/herself. Don't cut in abruptly or say to your spouse you don't have time to listen to complaints. Remember, if you don't work at making your marriage to be successful, it cannot.

"Be quick to hear and slow to speak."
(James 1:19)

Don't be defensive or raise a counter-accusation in your response. It is a sign of maturity to take responsibility for

Conflict Resolution

your actions. Even though, your actions might have been misconstrued by your spouse, since he/she got offended, you should take on the responsibility of clearing the air with a sincere apology.

Tell your spouse *"I am sorry"*. To say so does not reduce anybody. It rather brings healing to your hurting relationship. Show a sense of remorse and a willingness to change. To build your marriage, you must be willing to sincerely say you are sorry when your spouse is hurt, even when you feel you were right. It is very simple to say *"I am sorry"* and mean it! Remember many homes had crumbled because nobody is willing to say these very precious home-building words: *"I a m s o r r y"*.

Learn to forgive

Forgiveness is a common recipe in any stable and working marriage. Inability to forgive leads to bitterness, anger and unnecessary troubles. As a disciple of Christ, be ready to forgive your spouse seventy times seven times a day. When change does not come after several attempts, we have two options: either to be angry all the time or to work round the behaviour.

Every Marriage Can Work

How to fight fair

Sometimes, couples need to 'fight', but they should fight fair. Actually, couples do a lot of fighting over so many things, depending on their level of experience, maturity and understanding. Confronting your spouse over an issue that bothers you is good for your marriage. Don't brood over a hurt for so long if it does not go away, discuss it. Confront in love with the aim to build your relationship. Simon Presland listed ten ways on how to fight fair. I will list the ten points here: (used with permission).

How to fight fair[2]

1. Face your fear of confrontation.
2. Discuss the conflict as soon as possible.
3. State exactly what is bothering you.
4. Stick to the subject at hand.
5. If your spouse says you do, then it's true
6. Avoid generalizing.
7. Avoid personal insult and character assassination
8. Confront with truth. Affirm with love.
9. Listen to learn.
10. Confront to heal, not to win.

CHAPTER EIGHT

What is Love?

Love means so many different things to different people. When a boy says: "I love you" to a girl, and a girl says: "I love you" to a boy, it is certain they are not saying the same thing. Many times, a wife cries: "he doesn't love me", while the husband responds in amazement: "but I had been showing my love to you!"

The problem with loving is the HOW? That is why Paul admonished Titus to ask the aged women to teach the younger women **how** to love:

"The aged women likewise, that they be in behaviour as becometh holiness, not false accusers, not given to

Every Marriage Can Work

much wine, teachers of good things: that they may teach the young women to be sober, to love their husbands, to love their children, To be discreet, chaste, keepers at home, good, obedient to their own husbands, that the word of God be not blasphemed." (Titus 2:3-5)

Love can be taught. The teaching of 'how' has to do with experience and discoveries. That was why the aged women were to teach the younger women from their wealth of experience. However, if an aged woman who had a bad marriage teaches a younger woman how to love, the younger woman might find herself repeating that aged woman's errors. Be careful where you learn from.

From Paul's letter to Titus, if the aged women are to teach the younger women how to love their husbands, who then is to teach the younger men how to love their wives? I am sure we can easily deduce that the assignment of teaching the younger men should then fall on the aged men in the church.

In Greek, we have three main words that were used to describe love. The first is 'eros' which has to do with

What Is Love?

erotic love or lust. The second is 'phileo' which is the kind of love between brothers and sisters, parents and children. It is the filial love. The third kind of love is 'Agape'. 'Agape' is the God's kind of love. The love that loves the unlovable. It is sacrificial and knows no geographical or ethnic boundaries. Christians are to operate under this third kind of love.

Love is not an emotional feeling. Love is an action. Feelings can go, but love stays. People who suddenly woke up to declare *"I don't love her anymore"* or *"I don't love him anymore'* never really loved in the first place. They had emotional feelings and thought that was all about love. They were definitely not committed to real acts of loving.

Love is what you do, not just what you feel or say. Jesus advised his disciples in the following scriptures on how to love.

If ye love me, keep my commandments" (John 14:15)

"As the father hath loved me, so have I loved you: continue ye in my love. If ye keep my commandments,

Every Marriage Can Work

ye shall abide in my love: even as I have kept my father's commandments, and abide in his love. These things have I spoken unto you, that my joy might remain in you, and that your joy might be full. This is my commandment, that ye love one another, as I have loved you. Greater love hath no man than this that a man lay down his life for his friends, ye are my friends, if ye do whatsoever I command you."   *(John 15:9-14)*

Jesus' admonition to his disciples on how to love him was based on what to do to show their love. The words of Jesus in John 14:5 can be paraphrased like this: *"when I see you keeping my commandments, I know you love me"*. He went further in John 15:10 to say **"If ye keep my commandment, ye shall abide in my love"**. To 'abide in my love' means to 'stay in love with me'. *'Keeping my commandments is what keeps you in love with me'*. He also went further to show a demonstration of his own love for his friends. He laid down his life for his friends. Jesus' definition and description of love was based on what is done (action). To be in love with your spouse, you need to keep your spouse's 'commandments', i.e. doing those things that show your spouse your love. That is the only way you can love your spouse.

What Is Love?

"For God so loved the world, that He gave His only begotten son, that whosoever believeth in Him should not perish, but have everlasting life." (Jn. 3:16)

This scripture is the greatest love passage in the Bible. It shows the extent of God's love, and best illustrates what love is. From this great scripture, we can see that the real meaning of love is giving. There is no loving without giving. If the word 'giving' is to be removed from the above scripture, the whole verse becomes meaningless and starts raising questions. Without the word 'giving', John 3:16 will look like this:

"For God so loved the world, that He has (or kept) His only begotten son, that whosoever believeth in Him should not perish, but have everlasting life"

The first question that will come to anybody's *mind* from this incomplete scripture will be *"what has God done to show His love to the world?"* This is not an unusual question that we hear married people ask their partners all the time. The consideration of the fact that God gave his Son to redeem the dying world is a strong proof of God's love and a conviction to sinners to believe in the

Every Marriage Can Work

Son in order to have the eternal life God offers. So, the real definition of love is giving.

It is the consistent sacrificial giving that actually leads to a genuine emotional attachment and feeling which true love is. This level of love cannot be attained overnight. It does not come until couples have developed a deep level of intimacy through living together and consistently doing acts that means love to each other over a long period of time. One of the goals of marriage is for couples to attain intimacy. *"Therefore shall a man leave father and mother and be joined to his wife, and they shall become one flesh. And they were both naked, the man and his wife, and were not ashamed" (Gen. 2:24-25)*. There is a world of difference between just a feeling of attraction and intimacy. Anybody can suddenly develop an emotional feeling towards somebody of the opposite sex. This is not yet the true feeling of love. Such feelings can also suddenly fade away just like it developed. It is actually after couples are married that they start the journey towards intimacy. By the time they start living together, caring and meeting each other's emotional needs, intimacy begins to develop between them. This is the

What Is Love?

time they start having the true feeling of love. We can then say that giving leads to that deep sense of loving.

This fact can also be illustrated by parental love. It can be observed that parents love their children more than children love their parents. Is it surprising to you that your parents love you more than you love them and that you are going to love your children more than they will love you? The reason is not farfetched. It is because giving leads to loving. Little wonder Jesus said *"where your treasure is, there will your heart be also." (Matt 6:21).* Parents love their children so much because they had given so much to them. No child can recount how much his/her parents had given into his/her life. As a result of many years of consistent giving into the life of their children, the parents become so much emotionally attached to their children. This is the reason why parents don't feel much attachment to children they did not bring up themselves.

Giving leads to the true feeling of loving. The best way to give is giving what your spouse likes to receive as a gift. Giving what you like to be given as a gift to your spouse is not a reasonable giving. You'll end up using

Every Marriage Can Work

that gift yourself! God gave the world his Son to redeem the world because that was the greatest need of man at that time. God gave the world what the world needed and would treasure. That is the kind of giving that means loving.

According to Gary Chapman in his book: *'The Five Love languages'*, people give and receive love in five different ways:[3]

1. Giving quality time for sharing: Talking together, going out for recreation, eating out together, going on vacation/retreat together with the children or only the two of you etc.

2. The gift of physical touch: Holding hands, kissing, embracing, gentle massaging, running the hand through the hair, sexual intercourse, other love touches, etc.

3. Giving words of affirmation: Giving complements, encouraging words, words seasoned with salt (Col. 4:6), words of appreciation, words of commendation, etc.

What Is Love?

4. Giving and receiving gifts: Buying gifts, giving money, buying anniversary or birthday presents, designing special gifts, etc.

5. Giving acts of service: Washing dishes, cooking meals, taking out the garbage, washing clothes, ironing dresses, cleaning the house, washing cars, making the bed, planting flowers, perfuming the house, washing the bathroom, etc.

Find out which of these ways of giving means real love to your spouse and start loving (giving) from now. You will be surprised at the result you are going to get. What are you waiting for? Get set and GO!

CHAPTER NINE

The Duties Of A Husband

God, being the inventor and designer of the marriage union also provided a manual in His word that states how the marriage relationship between a man and a woman should be. The duties of both the husband and wife are clearly spelt out in the word of God. For marriage to work out as originally intended by God, husband and wife need to live up to their duties or responsibilities as commanded by God in the divine marriage manual (Bible). Remember, if you are going to enjoy your car to its maximum performance, you need to follow the guidelines of the manufacturers as stated in the owner's manual.

Every Marriage Can Work

Let's consider the duties of a husband:

1. Be the head

"For the husband is the head of the wife, even as Christ is the head of the church: and He is the Saviour of the body." *(Eph. 5:23)*

The husband is the head of his wife. He is not just to be the head as a title but dutifully.

The head leads. Wherever the head turns to, the body follows. The husband is to provide leadership for his family. The word of God also recommends that a man should practise leadership successfully, first at home before getting qualified to lead in the Church.

"……..For if a man know not how to rule his own house, how shall he take care of the church of God?"
(I Tim. 3:5)

The head also sees, hears, smells and speaks for the body. The man as the head is to provide vision for his family. The wife is to help or assist the husband fulfil the vision

The Duties Of A Husband

he had seen. The husband as the head is also to hear from God and smell danger for the family. The man as the head is the number one security man for his family. The man is to speak to God for his family and also speak against the enemies on behalf of his family.

To be the head is a duty a husband must fulfil for a successful marriage and family relationship.

2. Love your wife

"Husbands, love your wives, even as Christ also loved the church, and gave himself for it. So ought men to love their wives as their own bodies. He that loveth his wife loveth himself." (Eph. 5:25, 28)

"Husbands, love your wives, and be not bitter against them." (Col. 3:19)

Husbands owe it as a duty to love their wives. The kind of love a husband should have for his wife is the love that Christ had (and still has) for the Church and as a result gave himself for her. Jesus' love was a sacrificial love. True love is sacrificial. Giving is loving.

Every Marriage Can Work

Since husband and wife are one, it then follows that he that loves his wife, loves himself. When a man loves his wife, the wife will respond in submission and at the end of the day, the man would have done himself a lot of good by showing sacrificial love to his wife.

Men are also to love their wives as their own bodies. No man hates his body. When a man beats his wife, he is actually beating himself. Only mad men beat themselves on the streets! A man who loses his temper on his wife is actually less than being a man. He already lost control! Power is nothing without control.

If every man can possess the characteristics of love as written in I Cor. 13, the whole world will be in perfect peace and harmony. There will be nothing like wife-abuse, child-abuse, fighting and infidelity in the home.

Love is kind and suffers long. Love is neither proud nor behave itself unseemly. Love does not seek her own. It's not easily provoked and thinks no evil. Love rejoices not in iniquity but only rejoices in the truth. Love bears all things, believes all things, hopes all things and endures all things. Love never fails. It does not give up loving!

The Duties Of A Husband

For husbands to love their wives is more than a duty, it is a commandment. Every blessing of the covenant is tied to obeying God's commandments. For any man to enjoy true marital bliss, he must love his wife sacrificially as commanded by God.

Sacrificial love means a man should be ready and able to give up anything for his family to stay together. No other human relationship should be higher than his marital relationship. Love must involve sacrifice. First on the list of what to sacrifice for love is time. A man, who finds it difficult to sacrifice quality time to spend with his wife, can never reap the blessings of a successful and happy marriage.

For love to be real, it must be sacrificial. Men are not to love their wives as the first Adam loved his wife, but as Christ (the second Adam) loved the Church and gave Himself for her. The love of Christ is the standard of a husband's love for his wife.

3. Nourish your wife
"For no man ever yet hateth his own flesh; but nourisheth and cherisheth it, even as the Lord the Church." *(Eph. 5:29)*

Every Marriage Can Work

The husband is to nourish his wife. 'To nourish' means to cause to stay alive or grow by giving food, water etc. This means to bring up, care for and protect. Husbands are to nourish their wives just as they nourish their own bodies. The man is to lavish loving care on his wife. A man should endeavour to show interest on things that interest his wife. He should bring his wife up and seek for her spiritual, social and physical welfare. A loving husband should be able to know the emotional state of his wife and lovingly care for her.

4. Cherish her

"For no man ever yet hateth his own flesh; but nourisheth and cherisheth it, even as the Lord the Church."   *(Eph. 5:29)*

The husband is also to cherish his wife just as he cherishes his own body. To cherish means to care for tenderly. Husbands should relate with their wives with tenderness. They should not expect their wives to be like men! Women are completely different from men. According to the human anatomy, the physiology of a woman is strikingly different from a man's.

The Duties Of A Husband

When walking with their wives, husbands should slow down to allow their wives catch up with their speed. Raising the voice or speaking harshly should be avoided at home. Women are more emotional than men. Words convey a deeper meaning to a woman than it does to a man.

Men should be gentle with their wives just as they are gentle with their own bodies. No man bruises his own body but creams it, massages it and perfumes it. The same way, men should handle their wives with utmost care and gentleness.

5. Leave parents for wife

"For this cause shall a man leave his father and mother, and shall be joined unto his wife, and the two shall be one flesh." ***(Eph.5:31)***

It is the duty of the man to leave his parents. Many married men are yet to leave their parents. Marriage is for men that are already weaned from milk. A man who runs home every time to take instruction from his parents before taking any decision for his family is yet to leave.

Every Marriage Can Work

Leaving parents for wife also means a man should be independent financially from his parents. Money is a powerful tool of control. No man is truly independent from his parents until he is financially free from them.

A man who still lives under the same roof with his parents, or is still perpetually under the total influence of his parents is yet to leave.

Leaving parents means separation from them. Even though, a man should do his best to fulfil his filial obligations towards his parents, this does not mean that his home should be a mere extension of his parent's home. Marriage is for men, not boys.

Leaving parents is a duty which a man who is ready for successful marriage must perform. That is the recommendation in the owner's manual for marriage as commanded by God, the designer and the manufacturer of the marriage institution.

6. Cleave to wife

The Duties Of A Husband

"Therefore shall a man leave his father and mother, and shall cleave unto his wife: and they shall be one flesh."   *(Gen. 2:24)*

"For this cause shall a man leave his father and mother, and shall be joined unto his wife, and the two shall be one flesh"   *(Eph.5:31)*

After leaving parents, a man is required by God to cleave to his wife. When a man cleaves to his wife, they are joined together in spirit, soul and body, and they become one flesh. They become inseparable. They are glued together till death do them part.

It is a duty for the man to cleave to his wife. A man who once cleaved to his parents is now required to leave his parents and cleave to his wife. This means the man is to give his marital relationship a priority over his relationship with his father and mother. He should no longer take decisions alone or with his parents without his wife. He must not be joined in spirit, soul and body with someone else other than his wife. He is required to become so close and so joined to his wife so much that nobody can tell the difference between them.

Every Marriage Can Work

Cleaving is a herculean task for most men. That is why many marriages are not working the way God designed it to work. To cleave means there must be conscious steps to show and prove that husband and wife are now one flesh. The man is to consciously become close to his wife. His wife must be carried along in every decision making in his life.

Financially too, husband and wife should become one flesh. There should be no secrets between them. The man should allow his wife to know how much he is worth, just as the woman should also allow her husband to know how much she has. They should be naked and not ashamed of each other financially.

The word 'cleave to' also means 'to remain loyal' or 'remain faithful to'. Husbands have it as a duty to be loyal and faithful to their wives. To be 'loyal' means to be 'truthful', while to be faithful means there should be nobody else.

7. *Rule over his house*

The Duties Of A Husband

"One that ruleth well his own house, having his children in subjection with all gravity. For if a man know not how to rule his own house, how shall he take care of the church of God? (I Tim. 3:4-5)

The man being the head and the figure of discipline in the home is laden with the responsibility of maintaining law and order in his home. It is the man's duty to set rules for his family. He is however to show leadership in his home by example. Leadership by example is the highest form of leadership.

A man who cannot rule his house well is not to be allowed to set the rules in the church of God. Ruling means instilling discipline in his family, judging between the children and modulating the direction and character of his wife.

A man is to cultivate his wife into the kind of beauty he desires her to be. God never gave man anything in its finished state. Everything God gave man comes as raw materials. It is the duty of man to take the raw materials and process it into a finished product. Every man should

Every Marriage Can Work

labour to process his wife into his desired finished product.

8. Provide for His House

"But if any provide not for his own, and specially for those of his house, he hath denied the faith, and is worse than an infidel." (I Tim. 5:8)

It is the responsibility of the man to provide for his household. This means hard work. A man should train for a vocation or learn a skill so that he can feed his family, cloth them and shelter them. Whatever money a woman makes is just to assist the man in his duties.

A woman is not designed by God to be the bread winner for the family. The man is to go out, win the bread, and bring it home for his wife to distribute to the family. This does not mean that a woman should not work. A virtuous woman will do everything possible for her to assist her husband.

"Two are better than one." (Eccl. 4:9)

The Duties Of A Husband

It is even possible for a woman to be in a position where she can make more money than her husband. There is nothing wrong in that. What is wrong is if the man is not making any money at all. Such a man will lose respect from his wife. Most women can't handle a situation where they bring all the money needed in the family, and still have to submit to the man. At least, the man should be seen making efforts and trying to fulfil his obligations before he can earn some level of respect from his wife.

A man is also expected to provide security for his family. He is to protect and defend his wife especially from his own family members (her in-laws) and also from external aggressions.

When a man fulfils his duty as a provider to his family, his fatherly authority in the home is enhanced, and his self esteem increases. It is a thing of joy and fulfilment for a man to be able to provide for his home. Most men feel miserable when events turn otherwise. An understanding wife can always help her husband out of depression when he is financially incapable until the man is able to regain his much needed financial authority.

Every Marriage Can Work

When a man resigns to a life of pleasure and slothfulness just because his wife will always fill the gap, he may soon lose the marriage, the support, and may now be forced into getting a job. Why not get that job honourably now?

9. Honour His Wife

"Likewise, ye husbands, dwell with them according to knowledge, giving honour unto the wife, as unto the weaker vessel, and as being heirs together of the grace of life that your prayers be not hindered." (I Peter 3:7)

Men are to honour their wives as a matter of duty. God requires it from every man to honour his wife. Men are to dwell with their wives according to knowledge so that they can learn how to honour their wives. Every man needs to go to a 'school of marriage' for the purpose of knowing how to live and relate with his wife.

Men are to honour their wives as unto the weaker vessels. A man's muscles were not given to him by God for the

The Duties Of A Husband

purpose of beating up his wife. The muscles are for him to protect, care and honour his wife.

To honour is to show respect and for a woman, it also means to show affection. One of the things women thrive on is affection as discussed in chapter seven.

CHAPTER TEN

The Duties Of A Wife

1. Help meet

"And the Lord God said, it is not good that the man should be alone; I will make him an help meet for him." (Gen. 2:18)

A wife is a 'Help Meet' for her husband. God made the woman as a help meet for the man. A 'help meet' means a help that is 'appropriate', 'suitable for' and 'fitted to'. The woman was the appropriate, suitable and fitted help that man needed in the Garden of Eden. The situation is still the same till today. Where the man is weak, the woman is strong (to help the man's weaknesses). Where

Every Marriage Can Work

the woman is weak the man is strong. Eve was the appropriate companion Adam needed to curb his loneliness.

The woman is not a 'help mate', but a 'help meet'. This does not mean the woman is inferior to the man. All are equal before God. The woman is not inferior to the man. She only has a different role from the man.

Every Godly wife should aspire to complement her husband instead of competing with him. A woman should recognize her role as a help meet and fulfil it. When a woman competes instead of complementing her husband, divine order is disrupted and no marriage can be successful that way. Successful marriage can be a choice you made by your actions or inactions.

2. Submit to husband as to Christ

"Wives submit yourselves unto your own husbands, as unto the Lord." (Eph. 5:22)

Women are not to submit to men. Rather, it is wives that should submit to their own husbands. To submit means

The Duties Of A Wife

you allow him have the last word. Just as husbands are to love their wives as Christ loved the church and gave himself for her, so wives are to submit to their husbands as the church submits to Christ. A woman who cannot submit to her husband is yet to prove her submission to Christ.

A woman should not wait until she is convinced that her husband loves her before she submits to the husband. At least, somebody needs to start doing the right thing for the other to follow. Women who are married to yet-to-be saved husbands are admonished in 1 Peter 3:1 to be in subjection to their husbands. Their unbelieving husbands may be won to the Lord by their chaste conversation (behaviour).

3. Reverence Husband

"......and the wife see that she reverence her husband." (Eph. 5:33b)

It is a duty for a woman to reverence her husband. 'To reverence' means to show respect and exaltation. A woman who talks to her husband like she is talking to her

Every Marriage Can Work

servant does not reverence her husband. No man can truly love the wife who has no regard nor respect for him. No matter how a woman is highly placed in the society or opportuned in life, if she does not learn how to reverence her husband, she can never experience a truly successful marriage.

Sarah called Abraham Lord. She highly revered her husband (1 Peter 3:6). Queen Vashti disrespected her husband and she was removed as queen. Esther, a woman who abounded in quality took her place.

4. Home maker

"The aged women likewise, that they be in behaviour as becometh holiness, not false accusers, not given to much wine, teachers of good things; that they may teach the young women to be sober, to love their husbands, to love their children. To be discreet, chaste, keepers at home, good, obedient to their own husbands, that the word of God be not blasphemed."   *(Titus 2:3-5)*

"I will therefore that the younger women marry, bear children, guide the house, give none occasion to the

The Duties Of A Wife

adversary to speak reproachfully. For some are already turned aside after Satan." (I Tim. 5:14 -15)

Women are natural home makers. In Paul's letter to Timothy and Titus, he stressed the importance of instructing women on how to guide their house, love their husbands, love their children and keep the home. Women should use their natural abilities to make their homes a comfortable place for their husband and children. The Proverbs 31 woman is a home maker:

"She is not afraid of the snow for her household: for all her household are clothed with scarlet. She looketh well to the ways of her household, and eateth not the bread of idleness." (Prov. 31:21, 27)

It is the divine duty of the wife to make her home look presentable, her children well kept and her husband well taken care of. Women who don't know much about housekeeping should learn from the older women who are full of experience. Men generally are not gifted in such details as it is required in making the home. Women however, have been divinely endowed by God with such abilities.

CHAPTER ELEVEN

How To Change Your Spouse

Do you wish your spouse could change? How much have you tried to change your spouse? Many times, one partner desires a change in his/her marriage while the other partner appears not bothered. How can you influence your nonchalant partner to also seek for ways of improving on your marriage from his/her own side?

Some other times, partners are waiting for the other partner to change before making efforts to change. The wife is waiting for the husband to change while the husband is waiting for the wife to change. Nobody wants to take the first step, yet, somebody must take the first wisdom step.

Every Marriage Can Work

Change Yourself First
The best and sure way to change your spouse is to change yourself first. By changing yourself, you will eventually change your spouse. Start practising all the principles you have learned about marriage and in a short time, your spouse will follow suit. Don't wait for your spouse to change before you also change. Take the first step in the right direction. If you have a misunderstanding, be the first person to seek for reconciliation. Pick the phone and call. Give your spouse the benefit of a doubt. Relate with your spouse as if he/she has already changed. Expect your spouse to still make those mistakes while he/she learns a good example from you.

Reinforce the positive behaviours in your spouse. Encourage your spouse as he also starts taking positive steps to change. Give commendations and show appreciations. With God, nothing shall be impossible to her that believes.

Never Give Up
Don't ever give up on your partner. You have never tried enough until there is a desired change. At times, you need to engage the gear of endurance. When you are running

How To Change Your Spouse

out of endurance, you change to longsuffering. By the time your longsuffering is getting tired, you move to self-control! Before you exhaust all the gears of the fruit of the spirit (Gal.5:22-23), you would have driven your spouse to the destination of your desired change in him or her.

Pray for Your Spouse
There is nothing God cannot do. ***"The effectual fervent prayer of a righteous man is tremendous in its powers." (Jas. 5:16)***. God answers prayers if only you can ask in faith. Sometimes, your spouse might be under the influence of demonic manipulations. ***"We wrestle not against flesh and blood......" (Eph. 6:12)***. Engage the devil in a spiritual warfare over your spouse and you shall surely have your testimonies in Jesus' name.

CHAPTER TWELVE

Rekindling Love

You can rekindle your love with your spouse. Every love has the capacity to grow or die, depending on whether it is fanned up or not. God wants you to start experiencing heaven on earth in your home. It is possible for your marriage to work as God intended it.

The Principles of Decision and Discipline
Anybody can run a marathon race. Somebody who had never run a race all his life can run a marathon. What it takes is the principle of **Decision** and **Discipline**. If a man can arrive at a decision to run a marathon and gives himself to the discipline of training for the race, he can surely run the marathon and even win the race.

Every Marriage Can Work

What it takes for love to be rekindled in a marriage and for the marriage to be successful is a quality decision to have a successful marriage and a corresponding discipline of doing what it takes to achieve that. When you discipline yourself to keep your decision, you then become committed to having a successful marriage. Every couple can do it.

Decision + Discipline = Commitment.
Commitment is an important ingredient that must not be lacking for a marriage to be successful. Just like athletes commit themselves to training daily in their area of sport, so must husband and wife give themselves to the discipline of spending quality time together because it is a requirement for building a healthy family.

Make a Promise
Promises are words you are going to be committed to keep. It helps a lot to verbalize your decision. Call your spouse and make a promise to give your marriage a priority from henceforth. Promise to become committed to doing what will promote your marriage from now. Also promise to desist from doing those things that had been

Rekindling Love

pulling down your relationship. Rely on divine help and make up your mind to keep your promises.

Give Yourself No Alternatives
It takes dogged determination to work out your marriage. If love is going to be rekindled in your marriage, then you must come to a point where you have given yourself no other alternatives to making your marriage work. As long as you have alternative routes to fulfilling your marital needs and desires other than in your marriage, your union can never be successful. Also don't give yourself the alternative of patching it up. Make up your mind to enjoy your marriage and get committed to the discipline of your decision. It is possible!

Remain Faithful Even If .....
Your decision to pursue a successful marriage must be strong enough to still keep you faithful to your commitment even if:

- *your spouse is not yet cooperating*
- *you are not getting enough rewards for your sacrifices*
- *your spouse is not helping matters*

Every Marriage Can Work

- *your spouse is not keeping his/her side of the commitments*
- *your spouse becomes unfaithful.*

It should be noted however, that the last point is easier to handle for women than men, but if both partners can eventually arrive at this level of determination to pursue a successful marriage, they will surely enjoy heaven on earth in their marriage.

The Fear of God

Lastly, if you desire a rekindled love in your home for a peaceful and successful family life, you must have the fear of God. It's much easier for successful family relationship to happen where the fear of God is in place. It takes wisdom to build a house and the fear of the Lord is the beginning of wisdom (Ps. 111:10; Prov. 9:10). There is so much wisdom in living in the fear of God. The fear of the Lord is also the beginning of knowledge (Prov.1:7).

Marriage cannot run smoothly without both knowledge and wisdom.

Rekindling Love

"The fear of the Lord is a fountain of life, turning a man from the snares of death.." (Prov. 14:27)

"Through the fear of the Lord a man avoids evil." (Prov. 16:6)

"Humility and the fear of the Lord bring wealth and honour and life." (Prov. 22:4)

"Praise the Lord. Blessed is the man who fears the Lord, who finds great delight in his commands. His children will be mighty in the land, the generation of the upright will be blessed. Wealth and riches are in his house, and his righteousness endures forever." (Ps. 112:1-3)

The fear of the Lord alone can help any marriage to survive. Most of the vices that tear families apart are easily taken care of through the fear of the Lord. A man or a woman who fears God will not go into adultery, lie, cheat or abuse his/her spouse.

Since God hates divorce, (Mal. 2:16) a man or a woman who fears the Lord will not just wake up one morning and say "it is over" to his or her partner.

Every Marriage Can Work

One basic thing that is lacking in this generation is the fear of God. The God-factor is gradually being removed from the center of our society. God is being brushed aside in our daily decisions. That is why the centre can no longer hold. We all need to return to this place where God is feared and reverenced. God is a God of judgement. Before him, our actions are weighed. With the fear of God in your heart, you are surely on the path to a fulfilled family life. God bless you.

If you want to give your life to Jesus, say this prayer aloud:

"Heavenly father, I thank you for speaking to my heart. I know I am a sinner and I cannot help myself. I repent from my sins today. Forgive me lord and wash me with the blood of Jesus. Lord Jesus, come into my heart. I surrender my life to you from today.
Thank you lord for saving me. In Jesus name I pray (Amen)".

Rekindling Love

If you have said this prayer by faith in your heart, I want to assure you that you are now born again. Please write me and let us rejoice together.

You can also send me your questions and testimonies in your marriage.

References

1. Kay Arthur: *"A Marriage Without Regrets"*, Harvest House Publishers, Eugene, Oregon

2. Simon Presland: *"How To Fight Fair"*, Marriage Partnership, Summer 2001.
(Used with permission).

3. Gary Chapman, "The five love languages", Moody Press, Chicago, Illinois 60610-328.

Contact:

www.remioluyale.com
Email: info@remioluyale.com
Tel: +234 802 305 9599
Whatsapp: +2348023059599
Twitter: @remioluyale
Https://www.facebook.com/oluremi.oluyale

www.amazon.com/author/remioluyale

www.ingramcontent.com/pod-product-compliance
Lightning Source LLC
Chambersburg PA
CBHW032138040426
42449CB00005B/294